W9-CQZ-397

Animals I See at the Zoo/Animales que veo en el zoológico

PANDAS/ PANDAS

by/por Kathleen Pohl

Reading consultant: Susan Nations, M.Ed., author/literacy coach/consultant in literacy development

Consultora de lectura: Susan Nations, M.Ed., autora/tutora de alfabetización/ consultora de desarrollo de la lectura

WEEKLY READER®
PUBLISHING

Please visit our web site at: **www.garethstevens.com**
For a free color catalog describing our list of high-quality
books, call 1-800-542-2595 (USA) or 1-800-387-3178 (Canada).

Library of Congress Cataloging-in-Publication Data

Pohl, Kathleen.
    [Pandas. Spanish & English]
    Pandas/Pandas / Kathleen Pohl.
      p. cm. — (Animals I see at the zoo/Animales que veo en el zoologico)
    ISBN-10: 0-8368-8234-2 (lib. bdg.)
    ISBN-13: 978-0-8368-8234-6 (lib. bdg.)
    ISBN-10: 0-8368-8241-5 (softcover)
    ISBN-13: 978-0-8368-8241-4 (softcover)
    1. Giant panda—Juvenile literature. I. Title. II. Title: Pandas.
  QL737.C27P63518   2007
  599.789—dc22   2007021295

This edition first published in 2008 by
Weekly Reader® Books
An imprint of Gareth Stevens Publishing
1 Reader's Digest Road
Pleasantville, NY 10570-7000 USA

Copyright © 2008 by Gareth Stevens, Inc.

Editor: Dorothy L. Gibbs
Art direction: Tammy West
Graphic designer: Charlie Dahl
Photo research: Diane Laska-Swanke
Spanish translation: Tatiana Acosta and Guillermo Gutiérrez

Photo credits: Cover, p. 17 © Taylor S. Kennedy/National Geographic Image Collection;
title, pp. 9, 13, 15 © Tom and Pat Leeson; p. 5 © Aaron Ferster/Photo Researchers, Inc.;
p. 7 © Bruce Davidson/naturepl.com; p. 11 © Peter Oxford/naturepl.com; p. 19 © Lynn M.
Stone/naturepl.com; p. 21 © Jessie Cohen/Smithsonian's National Zoo/CNP/CORBIS

Printed in the United States of America

1 2 3 4 5 6 7 8 9 11 10 09 08 07

Note to Educators and Parents

Reading is such an exciting adventure for young children! They are beginning to integrate their oral language skills with written language. To encourage children along the path to early literacy, books must be colorful, engaging, and interesting; they should invite the young reader to explore both the print and the pictures.

The *Animals I See at the Zoo* series is designed to help children read about the fascinating animals they might see at a zoo. In each book, young readers will learn interesting facts about the featured animal.

Each book is specially designed to support the young reader in the reading process. The familiar topics are appealing to young children and invite them to read — and re-read — again and again. The full-color photographs and enhanced text further support the student during the reading process.

In addition to serving as wonderful picture books in schools, libraries, homes, and other places where children learn to love reading, these books are specifically intended to be read within an instructional guided reading group. This small group setting allows beginning readers to work with a fluent adult model as they make meaning from the text. After children develop fluency with the text and content, the books can be read independently. Children and adults alike will find these books supportive, engaging, and fun!

— Susan Nations, M.Ed., author, literacy coach,
and consultant in literacy development

Nota para los maestros y los padres

¡Leer es una aventura tan emocionante para los niños pequeños! A esta edad están comenzando a integrar su manejo del lenguaje oral con el lenguaje escrito. Para animar a los niños en el camino de la lectura incipiente, los libros deben ser coloridos, estimulantes e interesantes; deben invitar a los jóvenes lectores a explorar la letra impresa y las ilustraciones.

Animales que veo en el zoológico es una colección diseñada para ayudar a los jóvenes lectores a conocer a los fascinantes animales que pueden ver en un zoológico. En cada libro, los niños leerán interesantes datos sobre un animal.

Cada libro está especialmente diseñado para ayudar a los jóvenes lectores en el proceso de lectura. Los temas familiares llaman la atención de los niños y los invitan a leer una y otra vez. Las fotografías a todo color y el tamaño de la letra ayudan aún más al estudiante en el proceso de lectura.

Además de servir como maravillosos libros ilustrados en escuelas, bibliotecas, hogares y otros lugares donde los niños aprenden a amar la lectura, estos libros han sido especialmente concebidos para ser leídos en un grupo de lectura guiada. Este contexto permite que los lectores incipientes trabajen con un adulto que domina la lectura mientras van determinando el significado del texto. Una vez que los niños dominan el texto y el contenido, el libro puede ser leído de manera independiente. ¡Estos libros les resultarán útiles, estimulantes y divertidos a niños y a adultos por igual!

— Susan Nations, M.Ed., autora/tutora de alfabetización/
consultora de desarrollo de la lectura

I like to go to the zoo.
I see **pandas** at the zoo.

- - - - - - - - - - - - - -

Me gusta ir al zoológico.
En el zoológico veo
pandas.

Did you know a panda is not a bear? It just looks like a bear.

-- -- -- -- -- -- -- -- -- -- -- --

¿Sabías que un panda no es un oso? Sólo lo parece.

Pandas are black and white. They have white faces with black ears and black eye patches.

— — — — — — — — — — — — —

Los pandas son blancos y negros. Tienen la cara blanca, las orejas negras y marcas negras en los ojos.

eye patches/
marcas de los ojos

Pandas eat a lot! They eat tall grass called **bamboo**. In zoos, pandas eat apples and carrots, too.

- - - - - - - - - - - - - -

¡Los pandas comen mucho! Comen unas plantas altas llamadas **bambú**. En los zoológicos, los pandas también comen manzanas y zanahorias.

bamboo/bambú

11

They hold their food with their paws. Their front paws work like hands.

- - - - - - - - - - - - - -

Los pandas sostienen la comida con las zarpas. Usan las zarpas delanteras como si fueran manos.

The sharp **claws**
on their paws help
pandas climb trees.

Las afiladas **garras**
de sus zarpas permiten
a los pandas subir a
los árboles.

claws/garras

Pandas like to sleep
in trees.

- - - - - - - - - - - -

A los pandas les gusta
dormir en los árboles.

Pandas come from **China**, but only a few still live there. Zoos keep pandas safe.

Los pandas vienen de **China**, pero allí ya sólo viven unos pocos. Los zoológicos ayudan a proteger a los pandas.

I like to see pandas
at the zoo. Do you?

- - - - - - - - - - - - -

Me gusta ver pandas
en el zoológico. ¿Y a ti?

Glossary

bamboo — tall, hollow grass that grows in warm climates

China — a huge country in Asia

claws — the sharp, curved "toenails" on a panda's paws

pandas — animals from China that have thick, black-and-white fur and that look like bears

Glosario

bambú — plantas altas y huecas que crecen en climas templados

China — país muy grande de Asia

garras — las uñas afiladas y curvas de las zarpas de un panda

pandas — animales de China, con aspecto de oso, que tienen un pelaje grueso de color blanco y negro

For More Information/ Más información

Books/Libros

Arnold, Caroline. *Caroline Arnold's Animals: A Panda's World*. Mankato, Minnesota: Coughlan Publishing, Picture Window Books, 2006.

Bredeson, Carmen. *Zoom in on Animals! Giant Pandas Up Close*. Berkeley Heights, New Jersey: Enslow Elementary, 2006.

Edimat. *Oso panda y su cría*. Madrid: Edimat Libros, 2004.

Leeson, Tom and Leeson, Pat. *El oso panda*. San Diego: Blackbirch Press, 2002.

Ryder, Joanne. *Little Panda: The World Welcomes Hua Mei at the San Diego Zoo*. New York: Simon & Schuster, Aladdin, 2004.

Index/Índice

About the Author/Información sobre la autora

Kathleen Pohl has written and edited many children's books, including animal tales, rhyming books, retold classics, and the forty-book series *Nature Close-Ups*. Most recently, she authored the Weekly Reader® leveled reader series *Let's Read About Animals* and *Where People Work*. She also served for many years as top editor of *Taste of Home* and *Country Woman* magazines. She and her husband, Bruce, share their home in the beautiful Wisconsin woods with six goats, a llama, and all kinds of wonderful woodland creatures.

Kathleen Pohl ha escrito y corregido muchos libros infantiles. Entre ellos hay cuentos de animales, libros de rimas, versiones nuevas de cuentos clásicos y la serie de cuarenta libros *Nature Close-Ups*. Más recientemente, Kathleen ha escrito los libros de las colecciones *Conozcamos a los animales* y *¿Dónde trabaja la gente?* de *Weekly Reader*. Además, trabajó durante muchos años como directora de las revistas *Taste of Home* and *Country Woman*. Kathleen vive con su marido, Bruce, en medio de los bellos bosques de Wisconsin. Ambos comparten su hogar con seis cabras, una llama y todo tipo de maravillosos animales del bosque.